Collective Biographies

TEN AMERICAN
MOVIE DIRECTORS
The Men Behind the Camera

Anne E. Hill

Enslow Publishers, Inc.

40 Industrial Road	PO Box 38
Box 398	Aldershot
Berkeley Heights, NJ 07922	Hants GU12 6BP
USA	UK

http://www.enslow.com

For Brian, my favorite movie director

Library of Congress Cataloging-in-Publication Data

Hill, Anne E., 1974-
    Ten American movie directors : the men behind the camera / by Anne E. Hill.
      p. cm. — (Collective biographies)
    Includes bibliographical references and index.
    Summary: Ten biographies of American movie directors, including Frank
Capra, Alfred Hitchcock, Woody Allen, Francis Ford Coppola, Brian De Palma,
Martin Scorsese, George Lucas, Steven Spielberg, Spike Lee, and Quentin
Tarantino.
    ISBN 0-7660-1836-9
    1. Motion picture producers and directors—United States—Biography. I. Title:
10 American movie directors. II. Title. III. Series.
PN1998.2 .H55   2002
791.43'0233'092273—dc21

                                    2001006701
Printed in the United States of America

10 9 8 7 6 5 4 3 2 1

To Our Readers: We have done our best to make sure all Internet Addresses in this
book were active and appropriate when we went to press. However, the author and the
publisher have no control over and assume no liability for the material available on
those Internet sites or on other Web sites they may link to. Any comments or sugges-
tions can be sent by e-mail to comments@enslow.com or to the address on the back
cover.

Every effort has been made to locate all copyright holders of material used in this
book. If any errors or omissions have occurred, corrections will be made in future edi-
tions of this book.

Illustration Credits: Anne E. Hill, p. 50; Associated Press, pp. 14, 26, 32,
34, 41, 44, 52, 57, 62, 66, 70, 76, 80, 86, 88, 94; Associated Press,
UNITED ARTIST, p. 8; Library of Congress, pp. 16, 22.

Cover Illustrations: Associated Press, top right, bottom right, bottom left;
Library of Congress, top left.

Contents

Introduction

We all know the faces of famous actors and actresses. But many movie directors can walk down a street unnoticed, or at least less noticed than the men and women they direct on camera. That's because the work they do is behind the scenes. But it's every bit as important as that of big-name movie stars.

The men chronicled in this book, however, are noticeable—in most cases by both face and name—because they are the best at what they do. They have helped create the American cinema, the movies we all know and love.

Frank Capra directed the Christmas classic *It's a Wonderful Life*. Alfred Hitchcock is known for his suspenseful thrillers like *The Birds* and *Rear Window*. Woody Allen has made audiences laugh with his dry humor in classics like *Annie Hall*. Francis Ford Coppola introduced us to the lives of a Mafia family in *The Godfather* trilogy. George Lucas wowed audiences with his *Star Wars* series of films. Steven Spielberg brought us amazing characters like E.T. The Extra-Terrestrial and Indiana Jones.

Members of the group chronicled here have also learned from one another despite the fact that some of them have never met. Brian De Palma and Martin Scorsese have acknowledged being influenced by the work of Alfred Hitchcock. De Palma and Steven Spielberg are best friends who offer support when needed and criticism when it's called for. (Brian is even godfather to Steven's son, Max.) George Lucas directed his first movie for Francis Ford Coppola's film company, American Zoetrope. Lucas and Spielberg have collaborated on numerous films together. Spike Lee is a fan of Martin Scorsese. Quentin Tarantino's filmmaking style has also been compared to that of Scorsese, and he's been influenced by De Palma.

While these directors have all found considerable success in the medium of film, they've also encountered frustration—between critics and big studios, money and creativity, imagination and technology, even with themselves. Brian De Palma calls directing a schizophrenic profession. "Directing is standing behind the camera and watching what other people do. . . . You have to make things happen and then you have to sit back and see what you have created. In order to make it effective, you have to be detached."[1]

Director Francis Ford Coppola understands the clashing between creativity and money. He said, "You know what it's like to be a director? It's like running in front of a locomotive. If you stop, if you trip, if you make a mistake, you get killed. How can you be creative with that thing behind you? Every day I know it's $8,000 an hour. It forces me to make decisions I know will work. I can't afford to take chances."[2]

But the directors keep taking chances. They have all followed their own passions about theme, and many of their movies are intensely personal.

While males have dominated the movie-making industry, more and more women, like Amy Heckerling (*Fast Times at Ridgemont High, Clueless, Loser*), Jodie Foster (*Little Man Tate, Home for the Holidays*), and Penny Marshall (*Big, A League of Their Own, The Preacher's Wife*), have made strides in the movie industry and names for themselves as directors.

This book covers only ten great directors, but there are many more. The names Stanley Kubrick, James Cameron, Robert Redford, Oliver Stone, Cameron Crowe, Steven Soderbergh, Jonathan Demme, Mel Brooks, and M. Night Shyamalan have graced the marquees of very successful and influential films. What do they have in common with the ten in this volume? They are *all* great American movie directors.

1

Frank Capra

(1897–1991)

Frank Capra once said, "I know Americans better than people of any other country and by knowing them better I think I know what they laugh at and what should be laughed at."[1] But the man behind perhaps the most American of all films, the Christmas classic *It's a Wonderful Life*, wasn't born in America.

Francesco Capra was born in Sicily, Italy, on May 18, 1897, to Salvatore and Rosaria Capra. Twenty-three years later Francesco Capra became Frank Capra, an American citizen. When Frank was born he was so weak and dehydrated that he wasn't expected to live. But his grandfather knew not only that Frank would live but that he would be famous. The story handed down in the family is that

Frank Capra

Antonino Nicolosi, Rosaria's father, said, "You take care of that child. He's going to be known all over the world."[2]

Antonino was right, but it was hard for young Frank to believe he'd be anything but what his father was—a farmer. While it was a life full of hard work and little reward, the Capras did own a home and were always able to eat, due in large part to Frank's hardworking and resourceful mother. His father was known as lazy, but Frank still enjoyed his father's company.[3] He developed a love for the stories that his father told.

Frank's early childhood was spent roaming the streets of Sicily with his five older siblings and younger sister. In May 1903, just before Frank's sixth birthday, Salvatore and Rosaria and their four youngest children sold all of their belongings, left their small home and village, and boarded a ship bound for America. They were ready for a new life in California.

After a thirteen-day boat journey and an eight-day train ride, the Capras arrived in their new home in what is today the Chinatown section of Los Angeles. Back in the early 1900s, however, people of many different races and cultures inhabited the neighborhood.

Frank's father wanted him to go to school and get an education, but his mother thought her son should work.[4] It was decided that Frank would do both. Soon, Frank was selling newspapers when he wasn't in school. He later claimed he learned more selling newspapers than he did in his early years in the class-room.[5]

Before he even reached his teens, Frank knew that he needed to go on to high school if he wanted to succeed and rise above his family's blue-collar immigrant background. In order to attend Manual Arts High School, Frank worked not only as a paperboy but also as a janitor at the school. His hard work paid off and he was nearly a straight-A student through high school.

It was during his high school years that Frank began his show-business career. He played guitar for one dollar in downtown Los Angeles. Frank also joined the performance club, the Adelphic Society.

Movies were just being introduced when Frank graduated from high school in 1915. At the insistence of his art teacher, Rob Wagner, Frank went to see D. W. Griffith's movie epic of the Civil War and the Reconstruction era, *The Birth of a Nation*, which Frank called "the most important film ever made."[6] Nearly three years later, Frank went to Wagner for advice on a movie career.

Frank attended Throop College (now California Institute of Technology), majored in chemical engineering, joined a fraternity, and earned a Freshman Travel Scholarship prize, which allowed him to take a six-week trip around the United States. He had already accomplished more than his other family members while still a teenager. But Frank's enjoyment of his success was cut short by two things in late 1916 and early 1917: the death of his father in a farming accident and the declaration of war by the United States against Germany in World War I.

Frank's grades started slipping. Despite his efforts to graduate with a degree in chemical engineering, he didn't complete enough of his classes in the field and he received a general bachelor of science degree in September 1918.[7]

Instead of becoming an engineer, Frank Capra had a new passion: to become involved in movies. His choice was considered foolish and even Rob Wagner discouraged him from pursuing a film career. Capra, however, was determined to break into movies. Even though there weren't many jobs in this new medium, his persistence paid off.

In early 1920, Capra went to work for the Christie Film Company, known for its slapstick comedy. The job proved temporary but gave him some much-needed experience.

His odds of making it in movies, however, didn't always look as promising. Capra struggled to make ends meet. He worked as a tutor while writing ideas for film scripts. Then he went to work for the small company CBC that eventually became Columbia Pictures. He moved to San Francisco in 1920, which looked as though it might become the center of the moviemaking world.

Capra saw a newspaper ad placed by a Shakespearean actor named Walter Montague for a director to help make a screen version of his favorite poetry. The result of their collaboration was the short film *Fulta Fisher's Boarding House*. While Capra was proud of his interpretation of the Rudyard Kipling poem, he soon found that he wasn't considered a director in outside circles.

Instead of directing feature films, Capra served as a propman, editor, gagman, and assistant to the director on a series of films. While his roles were less glamorous, he met his future wife, actress Helen Howell, on the set. They were married on Thanksgiving Day 1923. (Unfortunately, the marriage lasted less than four years and the couple had no children.)

The center of the filmmaking industry was now Hollywood, so Capra and his wife moved there in January 1924. The move made his career. He became a gagman, coming up with jokes for Hal Roach's Our Gang (later known as The Little Rascals) series of films. It was through his work with Roach, producer/director Mack Sennett, and comedian Harry Langdon that Capra realized that he loved comedy. He later said, "I lean towards the comedy approach. My whole career has been making films laughing at ourselves (and myself)."[8]

Capra's first feature film, *The Strong Man*, was made in 1926 and was followed by *Long Pants* in 1927. Capra proved to be a competent director— perhaps too good for Harry Langdon's liking. Langdon wanted to make his own films, so he fired

Capra, who once again found work at Columbia Pictures.[9]

In the early 1930s, Capra managed to help the struggling movie company and make a major name for himself by directing films such as *Platinum Blonde, The Miracle Woman, The Bitter Tea of General Yen, American Madness,* and *Lady for a Day.*

But it was his 1934 film *It Happened One Night* that made Frank Capra famous. The film won five Oscars, including Best Picture and a Best Director award for Capra. His ability to get relaxed, natural performances from the actors made him one of the most sought after new directors in Hollywood. He worked with Gary Cooper, James Stewart, and Jean Arthur on films including *Mr. Deeds Goes to Town* (for which Capra won his second Best Director Oscar in 1936); *You Can't Take It with You* (for which he won his third Academy Award for Best Director in 1938); and *Mr. Smith Goes to Washington.*

Frank Capra's personal life was also on an upswing. He married Lucille Reyburn on February 1, 1932. They had four children: Frank, Jr., Sam, John, and Lulu. Capra was thrilled to be a father, and his joy might have translated into the films he later made.

At the start of World War II, Capra put his commercial film career on hold and, instead, made propaganda films for the Allies.

Even before the war, Capra's theme for his movies was clear. He wrote of this theme in his autobiography,

Frank Capra (left) shares a laugh with actor Jimmy Stewart during the filming of the 1946 film *It's a Wonderful Life*.

The Name Above the Title: "A simple, honest man, driven into a corner by predatory sophisticates, can, if he will, reach down into his God-given resources and come up with necessary handfuls of courage, wit, and love to triumph over his environment."[10]

Nowhere is this more evident than in Frank Capra's film *It's a Wonderful Life.* The holiday film tells the story of down-on-his-luck family man George Bailey who finds out what the world would have been like if he had never been born. It wasn't successful when it was released in 1946, but years later it has become a Christmas classic and perhaps Capra's most-loved film.

Capra made five more films after *It's a Wonderful Life* before retiring in 1961. Even though he was no longer making films, he wasn't forgotten. He received the American Film Institute Life Achievement Award in 1982. Frank Capra passed away in 1991.

Although he wasn't born in America, Capra embraced the lifestyle and values of his time and created some of the most distinctly American films of the Depression era 1930s and the war years of the 1940s. While his old-fashioned optimism is hard to come across in the films of the twentieth century, in 1986, Frank Capra remained optimistic about movies. "I say classics and great films are still to come. They will be made by the youth of today, and loving and praising the old films ought not to stop our belief that good ones are still to come."[11]

Alfred Hitchcock

2

Alfred Hitchcock
(1899–1980)

If Frank Capra tried to capture the goodness of people on film, Alfred Hitchcock found the dark side of human nature. "I don't want to film a 'slice of life' because people can get that at home, on the street, or even in front of the movie theater," Hitchcock said.[1]

But audiences embraced him nonetheless—and still do, years after his death. He has inspired countless modern-day filmmakers and his films have become even more popular as time goes by. "I'll tell you exactly why my father's work endures," his daughter, Patricia Hitchcock O'Connell, said. "Because he made his pictures for the audience, he didn't make them for the critics. And basically audiences do not change."[2]

Alfred Joseph Hitchcock was born the third child to William, a grocer, and Emma Hitchcock on August 13, 1899, in London, England. The Hitchcocks were a working-class Catholic family and all their children received a strict and religious upbringing.

So strict was his upbringing that at age four or five Alfred claims his father sent him to the police station with a note. "The chief of police read it and locked me in a cell for five or ten minutes, saying, 'This is what we do to naughty boys.'"[3] Alfred said he was never sure what he did wrong, and some doubt whether it even happened, but the experience affected him for years and even found its way into his moviemaking years later.[4] (He always distrusted policemen and one of his most popular themes was of men wrongly accused of crimes.) While strict and religious, the Hitchcocks loved theater. This also influenced Alfred.

As soon as he was old enough, William put his youngest son, whom he called Fred, into Catholic school. Fred hated his nickname and became known as Cocky in school. But he did not like that name either, so he later called himself Hitch.[5] Even as a youngster, Alfred liked to think for himself, laying the seeds for rebellion that came later. He admitted to not having many friends, instead he liked to watch and observe others and read his books. He especially loved American author Edgar Allan Poe.

Despite a love for reading, Alfred was not a stand-out student at St. Ignatius (from which he graduated in 1913). He did, however, enjoy science and art. He also spent time watching murder trials where he observed criminal behavior and developed an interest in crime and the criminal mind.[6]

Alfred attended the School of Engineering and Navigation, and as a teen went to work as a technical estimator for the Henley Telegraph Company in London. He also enrolled at the University of London where he studied art. Soon, Alfred moved to the advertising department at Henley where he was given the chance to draw. "[T]his work was a first step toward cinema," Hitchcock later said.[7]

Realizing that he wanted to draw and work in the motion-picture field, Hitchcock submitted his drawings to a production company that was opening in London called Paramount's Famous Players-Lasky. They immediately hired Hitchcock to illustrate the captions in silent motion pictures. Through his work there, he also learned to write scripts. At the age of twenty-three, Hitchcock was made an assistant director.

In 1925, at twenty-six, Alfred Hitchcock became a full-fledged director and took on his first project, *The Pleasure Garden*, which was filmed in Germany. Alma Reville, a writer and editor, was his assistant director on the project. The next year she became his wife. They were married for fifty-four years, until Hitchcock's death. They had one daughter, Patricia.

For the next thirteen years, Alfred Hitchcock honed his craft in England. He made twenty-three films with a variety of themes and styles. But his talent truly shone when he worked on thrillers like *The Lodger, Blackmail* (his first movie with sound), *The Man Who Knew Too Much, Sabotage, The 39 Steps, Secret Agent,* and *The Lady Vanishes.* "I am out to give the public good, healthy mental shake ups," he said. "Civilization has become so screening and sheltering that we cannot experience sufficient thrills at first hand. Therefore, to prevent ourselves [from] becoming sluggish and jellified, we have to experience them artificially."[8]

After fifteen years as Britain's foremost filmmaker, Hitchcock was ready to try his hand at American moviemaking. In 1939 he accepted an offer to direct a movie about the sinking of the *Titanic,* and he moved his family to the now-booming entertainment town of Hollywood, California. He said, "I wasn't the least interested in Hollywood as a place. The only thing I cared about was to get into a studio to work."[9]

And that's just what Hitchcock did for the next four decades, from the 1940s through the 1970s. The film about the *Titanic* was never made, but he did get the opportunity to make *Rebecca* in 1940 based on the novel by Daphne du Maurier. Hitchcock received an Academy Award nomination for directing and the film won Best Picture. It was a great beginning for him, and soon all of Hollywood's most famous actors and actresses wanted to work with him, including Grace Kelly, Kim Novak, Joan Fontaine, Ingrid Bergman, Cary Grant, Gregory Peck, Henry Fonda, and James Stewart.

In addition to hiring Hollywood's elite, Hitchcock had acting aspirations of his own, even though they were small. Beginning with *The Lodger,* he appeared briefly in each of his films, whether it was as a man walking down the street, on an elevator, at a party, boarding a train, or pictured in a photo album. He was said to be employed to "fill the screen."[10]

A relatively short man, Hitchcock tipped the scales at over three hundred pounds. In addition to filmmaking and his cameo appearances, he also became famous for his portly profile.

In the 1940s, Alfred Hitchcock made many films including *Suspicion, Spellbound,* and *Notorious.* He received another Academy Award nomination for 1944's *Lifeboat,* a film about a group of survivors from a torpedoed freighter, which was filmed entirely on board a small lifeboat.

By the 1950s, Alfred Hitchcock had found a home with American audiences. He was both an artist and a celebrity. He had money, two homes, land, cattle and oil interests, and Hollywood bargaining power. He also had developed a drinking problem.[11] Despite this, he made more and more films, and garnered more and more acclaim. He made some of his best-known films: *Strangers on a*

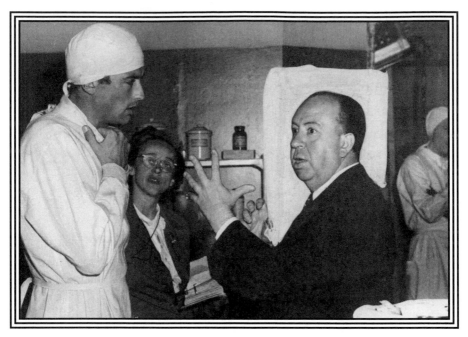

Alfred Hitchcock is giving direction to Gregory Peck during the filming of *Spellbound.*

Train in 1951 (in which his daughter, Patricia, costarred); *Dial M for Murder* (1953); *Rear Window* (1954); *To Catch a Thief* (1955); *Vertigo* (1958); and *North by Northwest* (1959).

His attention to detail and unusual camera techniques and angles made his filmmaking style unique. However, he did not develop a reputation for being too warm toward his actors. Actress Thelma Ritter, who costarred in *Rear Window*, said, "If Hitchcock liked what you did, he said nothing. If he didn't, he looked like he was going to throw up."[12]

The 1950s also saw Hitchcock taking on television, which was a new frontier for entertainment. His series of television thrillers aired from 1955 to 1965 (first called *Alfred Hitchcock Presents* and later retitled *The Alfred Hitchcock Hour*). Hitchcock helped select the stories and scripts, directed, and even introduced the show in a monologue. He said the most appealing thing about the television shows was "[t]he challenge of speed—most of the half hours were shot in three or four days. It was a complete change of pace, a different approach."[13]

Alfred was also changing pace—he was slowing down and made fewer films in the 1960s, but perhaps his most famous and his biggest commercial success was *Psycho*.[14] The film told the story of Norman Bates, a lonely man suffering from schizophrenia who owned a run-down motel. Hitchcock made four more films in the 1960s: *The Birds, Marnie, Torn Curtain*, and *Topaz*. He only made two movies in the 1970s before retiring from directing after 1976's *Family Plot*.

Now in his late seventies, Alfred Hitchcock had many health problems. And although he was housebound for nearly a year before his death on April 29, 1980, he was not forgotten in Hollywood or in his native England.

In 1979 he was honored with the American Film Institute Life Achievement Award. He was also knighted in 1980. Hitchcock had become known as the master of suspense; he was the most recognizable movie director.

With the introduction of VCRs in the 1980s, he had his own section of films, simply entitled "Hitchcock," in many of the early video stores. Director Aton Egoyan said, "Even more than the story and technical innovations, Hitchcock was able to put into the mainstream notions of perversity and subversive ideas."[15]

He also made the shortest Oscar acceptance speech, following his Irving G. Thalberg Memorial Award presentation from the Academy of Motion Picture Arts and Sciences in 1967. After receiving a standing ovation, Alfred Hitchcock simply said, "Thank you," and walked off the stage. Author Peter Bogdanovich wrote: "[W]hen the audience realized what he was doing, Hitch got a laugh and another hand. He didn't come back."[16]

3

Woody Allen
(1935–)

"I've never made a movie where scholars sat around and said, 'This ranks with the greatest,'" Woody Allen stated in 1995. "The trick is to have a great vision. That's not so easy."[1]

Woody Allen's vision has been making film-going audiences laugh for over three decades. His wit and humor blended with his own sarcasm and neuroses have created a unique flavor in the world of film. His controversial themes include sex and death, with Allen's characters worrying about both constantly.

Woody Allen was born Allen Stewart Konigsberg on December 1, 1935, to Martin and Nettie Konigsberg. The family lived in Brooklyn, New York, and Woody later joked that they were "dedicated to God and carpenting."[2] Actually, Woody's

Woody Allen

father held down a variety of jobs throughout Woody's childhood, among them a jeweler, taxi driver, bartender, and waiter. Woody's mother was a bookkeeper in a florist shop.

Woody's parents often fought. "They did everything except exchange gunfire,"[3] Woody recalled. His parents argued about money, especially because there never seemed to be enough of it. Despite their arguing and the fact that money was tight, the Konigsbergs had another child. Their daughter, Letty, was born when Woody was eight years old.

Even before Letty was born, Woody was fascinated by movies. He saw his first film, Walt Disney's *Snow White*, when he was three. He couldn't believe his eyes—the pictures on the screen were moving! He ran to touch the screen but his mother had to pull him back.[4]

From that moment on, Woody saw as many movies as possible. He fell in love with comedy at age seven when he saw Bob Hope in the movie *The Road to Morocco*. Woody was often first in line at the movie theater on Saturday mornings. He also enjoyed magic and even auditioned for a children's television magic show and, as a teen, performed at a resort club. Music also fascinated Woody. He loved jazz and played several instruments. He still plays the clarinet and soprano saxophone today.

With all of his interests, Woody was anything but ordinary as a child. He had a high IQ but didn't excel in school. However, recollections of his boyhood often appear in his movies. In school, he says, "I paid attention to everything but the teachers. As I've grown older, my life has developed a more tangible continuity with childhood than most people's. In my mind, it was only yesterday that I was standing in line to enter the school building."[5]

Going into Manhattan also had a profound effect on Woody and he fell in love with the city. It would later become the backdrop for his films as well as his longtime home.

But before he became one of the most acclaimed directors of all time, Woody had to get his start. At age sixteen, Allen Konigsberg changed his name to Woody Allen and began submitting jokes to a newspaper column. "I grew up taking great delight in comedy and making people laugh," he said. "I was always identifying with the comedian. It was a very painless way to get through life."[6]

The short, thin, redheaded boy had been making his teachers and classmates laugh for years with his gags and witty insights in assignments and reports. They weren't surprised when he was published. Woody worked part-time through his last two years of high school, selling gags and performing at clubs.

After he graduated from high school, Woody enrolled at New York University as a film major but only attended classes for a year. Instead, he turned his attention toward his budding comedy career. He was now writing for radio and continuing to sell jokes. At eighteen, he got a manager and began his career in earnest, writing for NBC's writers' development program.

As Woody Allen's career got underway, he also found love. He was introduced to Harlene Rosen through friends and the two were married on March 15, 1956. He was twenty and Harlene was seventeen.

Allen's parents worried that he would have a hard time supporting a wife. While the first few years of marriage were no doubt difficult financially, Allen was soon at the top of his profession. By 1960 he had written for comedian Sid Caesar's television show as well as *The Gary Moore Show*, and he had new managers—Jack Rollins and Charles Joffe. They later became his producers. But Allen was tired of television. He wanted to do stand-up comedy.

Largely autobiographical in nature, Woody's stand-up routines were embraced by nightclub audiences. He got even more material for his act after divorcing his wife in 1962. One of his routines included a story about his first marriage: His wife was an immature woman who used to burst into the bathroom and sink all his boats.[7] (Here, Allen was making fun of both his wife and himself. For who but someone even more immature than his wife would be playing with toy boats?)

Allen's comedy routines were recorded and sold as records, which brought him acclaim. His first, *Woody Allen*, was nominated for a Grammy award in 1964, followed by a second and third volume in 1965 and 1968.

But more importantly, his stand-up comedy brought him to the attention of producer Charles K. Feldman, who commissioned Allen to write a screenplay. Feldman even offered him a small role in what became Allen's first film, 1965's *What's New Pussycat?* Allen later said of the film, "If they had let me make it, I could have made it twice as funny and half as successful."[8]

But success was waiting for Woody Allen. The year 1966 was big for the thirty-year-old. He made his directorial debut with *What's Up, Tiger Lily?*—a kind of Japanese James Bond film. While it did not make as much money as his first film, it developed a cultlike following.

Allen also saw the opening of his first Broadway play, *Don't Drink the Water.* It ran for over a year and inspired movie and television versions. He also married actress Louise Lasser, and although the marriage lasted only three years, she appeared in his first three hit comedies: *Take the Money and Run* (1969); *Bananas* (1971); and *Everything You Always Wanted to Know About Sex but Were Afraid to Ask* (1972).

Woody Allen was now a writer and director and in charge of production, but he was not always in control. That was part of the beauty of his filmmaking. He said, "I don't rehearse a film. I never know where I'm going to put the camera. Funniness is organic, like sitting around with a lot of people when something loopy happens. What you write is not what you shoot at all. I've shot the middle of a movie again and again and eventually put it somewhere else."[9]

But whatever his style, it worked. The 1970s were Allen's heyday for comedy. His hits included 1977's smash hit *Annie Hall*. The film tells the love story of two neurotics, comedian Alvy Singer (whom Allen played) and wanna-be singer Annie Hall. The film won four Academy Awards, including Best Picture, Best Actress, and two for Allen: Best Director and one he shared for writing the screenplay. Best Actress winner Diane Keaton, who played Annie Hall, became closely linked with Allen both professionally and romantically through much of the 70s.

After *Annie Hall* in 1977, the inventive Allen next turned to a drama, *Interiors*, and mixed the two throughout the 1980s. He made such acclaimed films as *Manhattan, Stardust Memories, A Midsummer Night's Sex Comedy, Broadway Danny Rose, The Purple Rose of Cairo, Hannah and Her Sisters* (for which he won another Academy Award for writing the screenplay), and *Radio Days*, which was based on Allen's own childhood.

In the midst of all his moviemaking, Allen also fell in love with actress Mia Farrow. Because of his relationship with her, Allen also came to realize that children were very important to him. Woody Allen had always said he did not have time for kids of his own, but Farrow had seven, both natural and adopted kids, when she met him. They stole Allen's heart. He said, "Only after being around Mia have I

Woody Allen's unique approach to film has been examined by the most prominent film schools in the country.

seen that children are so meaningful to people in helping define their lives. . . . Once you have a child, it is so powerful an experience, it's impossible not to put it first. It eclipses others by far. It's a bigger kick getting a laugh from the baby than it is from a whole audience."[10] They adopted one child together, daughter Dylan, and had another, son Satchel, together.

Unfortunately, the relationship and parenting lives of Farrow and Allen did not end happily. Although they made many films together and were a couple for more than a decade, the two had an ugly custody battle over their children in the early 1990s. Allen began a romance with Farrow's adopted daughter Soon-Yi Previn and they married in 1997. They have since adopted two daughters of their own.

Woody Allen continues to surprise audiences. His screen-writing partner, Marshall Brickman, said that for Allen "self-expression is a large part of the equation. He doesn't buttonhole people to ask, 'What kind of movie should I make?'"[11]

Despite Allen's ability to bankroll his films for millions of dollars, he employed a wobbly handheld camera for his comedy *Manhattan Murder Mystery*, which reunited him professionally with Diane Keaton. He even surprised movie audiences with a musical comedy—1996's *Everyone Says I Love You.*

Woody Allen continues to make movies and music today, playing with a jazz band every week in New York City.

Francis Ford Coppola

4

Francis Ford Coppola
(1939–)

When Francis Coppola was just ten years old, he came down with polio. Confined to his house for nearly a year, he discovered his passion—making movies. Bored and lonely, the youngster put on performances with a tape recorder, a 16-mm film projector, puppets, and the Coppola family television.

He recovered from his illness, but he was changed for good. He later explained that while he was sick he had decided to have his own movie production company some day "where we could work together like children, with music, puppets, scenery, lights, dramatic action, whatever we wanted to do."[1] Twenty years later, that was exactly what he did.

Francis Ford Coppola was born in Detroit, Michigan, on April 7, 1939, the second of three children born to Carmine and Italia Coppola. At the time of Francis's birth, his father was a conductor, composer, and flutist with the Detroit Symphony Orchestra. His mother was an actress.

Not long after Francis was born, the Coppolas moved to the Queens section of New York City so that Carmine could join the prestigious NBC Symphony Orchestra. Growing up in New York was an adventure and there was no shortage of things for Francis and his older brother, August, to do. They loved going to the movies. But Francis was not just content sitting in his seat and watching the films, he also became fascinated by the technology used to make them. He played with as many gadgets as he could find and even edited films shot by friends of the family.

When he was not going to the movies or building things, "Science," as Francis was nicknamed, was following in his father's musical footsteps. He learned to play the tuba and was so impressive that he received a music scholarship to the New York Military Academy when he was a teenager. But movies and theater were far more interesting to Francis, and after a year and a half at the school, he dropped out. Unhappy and unsure what to do next, Francis returned to New York City. He finished his high school education at various high schools in Queens and continued playing the tuba.

Francis began writing plays when he was sixteen, which led to a partial theater-arts scholarship to Hofstra University after he graduated from high school in 1956. "Hofstra was significant for me because after a career of going to many, many high schools . . . and being the odd man out and kind of a boy scientist, my first year of college consisted of having a group of friends in the theater-arts department and actually going through four years at the same school."[2]

While he loved theater, Francis knew his future lay in film. So he sold his car while he was still in college in order to buy a 16-mm movie camera and made his first short film. It told the story of a woman and her children, whom she takes to the country for a trip. She then loses them.

After he graduated from Hofstra University with a degree in drama, Francis Coppola left the East Coast for the West and the University of California at Los Angeles Film School (UCLA). He threw himself into making student films and even found work assisting director Roger Corman. Coppola helped the low-budget film master with scripts, dialogue, sound, and producing chores. He convinced Corman to let him make his own movie. In 1963, *Dementia 13* directed by Francis Ford Coppola was released. The twenty-four-year-old's horror film revolved around a series of ax murders at an Irish castle. He shot it in just a few days while helping Corman make *The Young Racers* in Ireland.

But his good luck did not end there. Coppola married his wife, Eleanor, around the time he was assisting Corman. Their first son, Gian-Carlo, was born in 1963 and their second, Roman, was born in 1965. Daughter Sofia (who later became an actress and director) was born in 1971.

Fortunately for Coppola, his career was starting to take off as his family grew. After winning the Samuel Goldwyn Award for most outstanding screenplay by a UCLA student, he was offered a position as a contract writer.

In 1966 he got the opportunity to direct a film he wrote—*You're a Big Boy Now*. He also developed a business strategy that set him apart from the big studios and made him independent. He explained, "I wanted to write a sort of innocent *Catcher in the Rye* coming-of-age story about a kid like me. But I was under contract to Seven Arts, so if I wrote an original screenplay they would own it and wouldn't let me direct it. So I bought the rights to a novel, *You're a Big Boy Now*, which had a similar premise. . . . I used that leverage to talk them into letting me direct it."[3]

Twenty-seven-year-old Coppola won acclaim for the film and earned his master's degree in fine arts from UCLA. (He submitted the film as his thesis.)

It seemed as though Coppola had arrived on the Hollywood scene when he learned that the next picture he would direct would be the musical comedy *Finian's Rainbow*. Anxious to impress his musician father, Coppola agreed to do it but soon learned it was not going to be as he imagined. "I discovered that it was going to be really low-budget. [Warner Brothers] figured it would use the sets from *Camelot*, get a young director who knew how to work cheap, talk Fred Astaire into being in it, and do the whole picture in 29 days. . . . Now I realize I could've made it much, much better if I had done it because they schmaltzed it up. . . . But I learned: Always do your own postproduction."[4]

After his bad experiences on the set of *Finian's Rainbow*, Coppola decided to create his own production company, American Zoetrope, in 1969. The company's first film, *THX 1138*, was directed by another soon-to-be big name, George Lucas.

Although Coppola and Lucas have been friends ever since, Zoetrope has gone through ups and downs. After a series of failures, the film studio plunged into debt, and Coppola was unable to "transform the system by showing a love for writers and directors" as he had always hoped.[5]

While he tried to pay off his debts, Coppola agreed to direct and cowrite the script of the 1972 film version of author Mario Puzo's *The Godfather*. (During this time Francis also won his first Oscar for Best Original Screenplay for 1970's *Patton*.)

The Godfather, the Italian-American epic about a Mafia crime family became hugely successful and was widely received, due in large part to Coppola's vision of portraying cold-blooded killers humanely. Paramount executive Robert Evans said that Coppola "[k]new the way these men ate their food, kissed each other, talked. He knew the grit."[6]

The Godfather won Academy Awards for Best Picture, Best Actor, and Best Screenplay (an award Coppola shared with Puzo). Coppola went on to win two more Oscars (for Best Director and Best Adapted Screenplay) for the 1974 sequel, *The Godfather Part II.*

Although it seemed Zoetrope had escaped financial catastrophe after the success of the *Godfathers* and 1973's *American Graffiti,* Coppola struggled through on-set catastrophes of the 1979 film *Apocalypse Now.* He went broke after 1982's *One from the Heart.* The film exceeded its budget by millions and did not succeed at the box office. It took Coppola more than a decade to pay off the millions of dollars he owed.[7]

But he kept working, making the 1980s teen films *The Outsiders* and *Rumblefish,* the jazz flick *The Cotton Club,* and the fantasy film *Peggy Sue Got Married,* which costarred Coppola's nephew Nicolas Cage.

In 1987, Coppola and his wife suffered a tragedy when their oldest son died in a boating accident on the set of *Gardens of Stone.* Coppola finished the film and made others, including *Tucker* and *Bram Stoker's Dracula,* before making *Jack* in 1996. *Jack* tells the story of a boy with a rare disease, which makes him age at an incredibly fast rate. This film is considered

Francis Ford Coppola reveals a slight smile as he arrives at Cannes Film Festival.

a tribute to Coppola's son, Gian-Carlo, and his son's daughter, Gia, who was born after her father's death.

In 1998, Coppola won the Director Guild of America's D. W. Griffith Award. He drove down to Hollywood to accept the award from his Napa Valley, California, estate and winery he owns with his wife. In addition to wine making, he also enjoys cooking and writing. "My great gift is that I'm really a writer," he said. "I have felt frustrated over not being able to do it in the past, except for *The Conversation*. Now I can."[8]

Francis Ford Coppola continues to make films that are important to him personally, but he has become more selective about his projects. "When you're young, you make any movie, just to make a movie. When you're old, there must be something that interests you. I think I'm there now," he says.[9] "That's the Holy Grail, whether you're Martin Scorsese or some 24-year-old kid borrowing money from your uncle," he said. "You want to make personal films."[10]

5

Brian De Palma
(1940–)

"I want to be *infamous*. I want to be *controversial*. It's much more colorful," Brian De Palma has said.[1] And, indeed, many of Brian's movies have flown in the face of conventional Hollywood. While his friends and fellow moviemakers Francis Ford Coppola, Martin Scorsese, George Lucas, and Steven Spielberg have gone more mainstream, De Palma has always been on the edge of what's acceptable, but it's exactly where he wants to be.

Brian De Palma was born on September 11, 1940, in Newark, New Jersey, to Dr. Anthony and Vivian De Palma. He was the De Palmas' third son, joining older brothers Bruce and Bart. Shortly after Brian was born, his father, an orthopedic surgeon, went away to fight in World War II. When he

Brian De Palma

returned, the family moved to Philadelphia, Pennsylvania, where he headed the department of orthopedic surgery at Jefferson Medical College. He worked long hours, so the De Palma boys were left to the care of their mother.

Although the De Palmas did not have to worry about money, the sons were not allowed to take their privileges for granted. Brian sold newspapers on the streets near their home and also worked as a dockhand when his family summered at the New Jersey shore.

His menial jobs, however, could not hold a candle to his father's work of operating on bones, amputating limbs, and installing new ones. Brian was fascinated with his father's work and it influenced the movies he later made.

Brian attended a Quaker school, Friends Central, in Philadelphia, where he struggled to be noticed in the shadows of his older brothers. Brian was very socially active—he was president of the Social Committee and the Science Club, played varsity tennis and football, worked on the yearbook, was a member of the chess team, and acted in school productions. Yet he still felt his accomplishments did not measure up to those of his brothers, especially Bruce, who had won third place in the Philadelphia Science Fair and was generally regarded as his mother's favorite.[2]

Motivated for some attention and glory of his own, Brian entered science fairs as well, and won first prize in the Delaware Valley Science Fair and second prize in the National Science Fair. Thus began a lifelong obsession with science and technology that still continues for Brian. It's what keeps him motivated to make movies today. "I'm the guy who used to build computers," he said in 1998. "I'm right at the cutting edge of what's going on in the whole new revolution. I watch this stuff all the time and I'm fascinated every time some new development happens—and it happens every other month in this industry."[3]

Brian's parents separated when he was a teenager, shortly before he left for college, and they later divorced. Brian left Philadelphia for New York City's Columbia University. He intended to be a physics major but changed his mind during his sophomore year. Instead, he decided he wanted to join the Columbia Players theater troupe and direct some films. But he soon learned that undergraduate students were not allowed to direct movies. Not one to give in easily, Brian struck out on his own. He bought a 16-mm camera and decided to make his own forty-minute short film entitled *Icarus.* Later he called the film "pretentious and disastrous, but nonetheless, a beginning."[4]

With his science and technical background, Brian opted to be the cameraman and brought in a director to help with the picture. After the director quit, Brian took over in the director's chair. He never looked back. He made a couple more student films that he financed by selling his science equipment and getting some money from his parents. Brian was already dedicated to his chosen craft.

He studied the masters, including Alfred Hitchcock, whom critics have claimed that Brian has been too heavily influenced by and followed too closely. But Brian wanted to be a visual director, much like Hitchcock. "If you're working with this type of visual storytelling, you're going to be using material Hitchcock has used before," he later said.[5]

Brian's 1962 film, *Wotan's Wake*, won a $1,000 prize and earned him a writing fellowship toward a master of fine arts degree at Sarah Lawrence College. There, twenty-three-year-old Brian got the chance to make his first full-length film, *The Wedding Party*. He cast aspiring actors Robert De Niro and Jill Clayburgh in the film, which was not released until 1969.

In the meantime, he got work directing a few more short films and documentaries, including *Mod* about the rock groups The Who and The Rolling Stones; *Bridge That Gap*, a documentary about African-American politics; and *The Responsive Eye*, which chronicled the opening of the Kino exhibition at the Museum of Modern Art in New York City.

The short film and documentary work De Palma took on during the mid-1960s financed making his own films, which he both wrote and directed, in the late 1960s—*Murder a la Mod, Greetings,* and *Hi, Mom!* While none of these films earned him overnight success, they did get him noticed, and thirty-year-old De Palma was asked to film his first big-budget picture, *Get to Know Your Rabbit*, for Warner Brothers Studios in 1972.

Unfortunately, the now die-hard New Yorker's first taste of Hollywood was sour. De Palma clashed with the film's star, television actor Tommy Smothers, and De Palma was fired. He returned to New York and the independent filmmaking he now knew well. But with one difference: His films became more violent in nature and filled with disturbing and dark themes. He also developed a cult following after his 1970s' films *Sisters*, *The Phantom of the Paradise*, and *Obsession*.

In 1976, De Palma directed the successful adaptation of the Stephen King thriller *Carrie*. Suddenly, he was a legitimate filmmaker in the eyes of the public and the critics. For years he had struggled with public success. As writer Julie Salamon wrote in her book *The Devil's Candy*: "He [De Palma] wanted to be recognized as an artist by the critical establishment, and he wanted to achieve box office success. Yet his most personal films could never have the mass appeal of more conventional movies."[6]

One of De Palma's more unconventional and deeply personal movies was the partly autobiographical *Home Movies*, which was released in 1979, and was based on his childhood. *Home Movies* was the second movie to feature actress Nancy Allen. They were married the year the film was released, but they divorced in 1983.

By this time De Palma had directed several more movies, including the well-received *Dressed to Kill*, the thriller *Blow Out*, which starred a young John Travolta, and *Scarface*, which was nearly given an X-rating by the Motion Picture Association for its extreme violence. His 1984 movie *Body Double* was also highly controversial because it dealt with violence and pornography.

Tired of fighting against the conventional Hollywood standard, De Palma spent the later half of the 1980s shattering the image that he was Hollywood's bad boy. He made the 1986 comedy *Wise Guys*, which opened with the line: "You talking to me?"—a line taken straight from *Taxi Driver* and a nod to the success of his friends Martin Scorsese and Robert De Niro. De Palma also made the incredibly popular *The Untouchables*, which won actor Sean Connery the Academy Award for Best Supporting Actor.

Riding high on the critical and commercial success of *The Untouchables*, De Palma's good mood changed after a string of disappointing films in the late 1980s and early 1990s: *Casualties of War*, *Bonfire of the Vanities*, and *Raising Cain*. (The making of *Bonfire of the Vanities* became the subject of Julie Salamon's book *The Devil's Candy*.)

Fortunately, his personal life was in an upswing. De Palma met producer Gale Anne Hurd. They married in 1991 and their daughter, Lolita, was born later that year. The marriage did not last, but De

Brian De Palma with his relative and author of *Ten American Movie Directors*, Anne E. Hill.

Palma remarried to ballet dancer Darnelle De Palma and had another daughter, Piper, in 1996. He is now single again.

In 1996, after the success of *Carlito's Way*, De Palma made the summer blockbuster *Mission: Impossible*, his most financially successful film to date. He followed it with the more mild successes: *Snake Eyes* in 1998 and *Mission to Mars* in 2000. Currently, he is working on *Femme Fatale*, a thriller starring Antonio Banderas.

When asked how he chooses the films he makes, De Palma said, "There's a whole swirl of emotions that go into the decision. A lot of times you make movies because you don't want to think about what's happening with the movie you just made. You don't want to think about the reviews out there or about how you're going to survive the pummeling that you're getting."[7] Although the critics have not always been friendly to De Palma, he has not gone out of his way to give interviews or go to premieres. He has never enjoyed the Hollywood lifestyle.

De Palma's film career has been filled with joyful ups and painful downs, but he has remained true to himself and his way of moviemaking. "The thing you can determine from me is that I never [cared] what anybody thought."[8]

As for his recent successes, Brian De Palma says, "It's better to make them at the end rather than at the beginning. And I'm full of ideas, more ideas than I can ever make."[9]

Martin Scorsese

Martin Scorsese
(1942–)

Like the films of his good friend, Brian De Palma, Martin Scorsese's films became popular in the late 1960s and early 1970s. In fact, Scorsese, De Palma, George Lucas, Francis Ford Coppola, and Steven Spielberg are often grouped together as the definitive moviemakers of their generation.

What sets Martin Scorsese apart from the rest is the influence he has had on the independent, or indie, film. "[H]e pioneered a new street cinema," said author Peter Biskind. "He worked on his own terms and made the kind of films he wanted to make. . . . He fathered the independent film we have today."[1]

Martin Scorsese was born on November 17, 1942, in Flushing, New York, to Charles and

Catherine Scorsese. He was raised in the Little Italy neighborhood of New York City. The Scorceses were Catholic and Martin's first aspiration in life was to be a priest. While he waited to enter the priesthood, young Martin occupied himself by going to the movies and watching television. Plagued by severe asthma, he could not participate in sports and other activities that kids his age liked to do.

When he was outside in his neighborhood, Martin was influenced by what he saw. He later said, "Violence will settle something, but only for a while. I saw that all my life, growing up. I saw people taking care of things by violence."[2] The violence Martin saw stayed with him and influenced the films he would one day create.

As a teen, Martin entered the seminary. But a year later he dropped out to follow what had become his obsession: film. He entered the Film School at New York University (NYU) and began studying the art form he'd come to love. Alfred Hitchcock, Hollywood musicals, and the classic westerns of director John Ford particularly intrigued him. Critics later said that he created a kind of new urban western with his films.[3]

It was clear almost from the beginning of Martin's filmmaking in the mid-1960s that he had immense talent. He won many awards for his short films at NYU, and even won the Producers' Guild Award for best student film in 1964 for *It's Not Just You, Murray!*

After graduating, Scorsese stayed on at NYU to teach other novice filmmakers. He also married aspiring actress Laraine Marie Brennan on May 15, 1965. Their marriage, however, only lasted a few years.

Scorsese started his career with some more short films. His first feature film was 1969's *Who's That Knocking at My Door*. Largely autobiographical, the film was produced by one of Scorsese's teachers at NYU.

The late 1960s was a period rich with emotions and endless possibilities for films. The Vietnam War was in full force, and after four students were killed at Kent State University while protesting U.S. involvement in the war, Scorsese and some of his students formed the New York Cinetracts Collective and filmed student protests to the war. The result of their efforts was 1970's *Street Scenes*.

Martin Scorsese was not just interested in directing, however. He worked as a film editor on the documentary *Woodstock* and also did some television work before deciding he needed to move to Hollywood. While New York had a large piece of the entertainment pie, its center was Los Angeles.

When he arrived there, he worked with producer and director Roger Corman, as Francis Ford Coppola had. Corman allowed Scorsese to work on *Boxcar Bertha*, a Bonnie-and-Clyde type of gangster film based on the memoirs of Bertha Thompson.

Scorsese was grateful to have gotten his start in Hollywood, but he could not keep the streets of New York out of his mind. Fortunately, aspiring actor Robert De Niro, one of Scorsese's friends from Little Italy, was also in Hollywood.

The first of their many successful collaborations was *Mean Streets*, which Scorsese also wrote and appeared in. The film tells the story of young Italian-Americans in a tough neighborhood who "would hardly think of themselves as criminals, although at one level or another they are all connected with crime. . . . What eventually pulls them apart is a stumbling for self-respect that must be expressed in violence."[4]

Scorsese spent the 1970s creating feature films and documentaries, both personal in nature and largely based on his Italian-American upbringing. His biggest hit of the 1970s was *Taxi Driver*, which is considered by many critics to be the best film of the decade.[5] Scorsese was introduced to the writer of *Taxi Driver*, Paul Schrader, by Brian De Palma, who was collaborating with Schrader on his film *Obsession*. While the budget for *Taxi Driver* was low, Scorsese and Schrader were determined to make the film. Scorsese admits that he saw the film as "a labor of love rather than any kind of commercial success."[6]

"The whole film is very much based on the impressions I have as a result of growing up in New York and living in the city," he said in his book *Scorsese on Scorsese*.[7] *Taxi Driver* tells the story of

Martin Scorsese made his mark in film with *Taxi Driver* starring Robert De Niro and Jodie Foster.

Vietnam veteran and New York City taxi driver Travis Bickle (played by Robert De Niro) who becomes a murderer. The film was awarded the International Grand Prize at the Cannes Film Festival.

After the success of *Taxi Driver*, Scorsese was riding high, but he came crashing down with his next film, *New York, New York*, starring De Niro and Liza Minnelli.

Scorsese was having troubles in his personal life as well. He had had two failed marriages, first to Laraine Brennan (with whom he had daughter Catherine Terese Glinora Sophia), then to writer Julia Cameron (with whom he had daughter Domenica Elizabeth in 1976). He had other relationships, with producer Sandy Weintrub and actress Liza Minnelli, and the failure of these, along with drug problems and the poor response to *New York, New York*, led to Scorsese's hospitalization. The film's failure also convinced him to finish off the decade making documentaries.

But Scorsese did not stay away from feature films for too long, and he did not stay single either. He married for the third time on September 29, 1979, to actress Isabella Rossellini.

His new film was 1980's *Raging Bull*, the story of boxer Jake LaMotta. Robert De Niro gained more than fifty pounds to portray the boxer in LaMotta's later years, proving his dedication and his acting skills. He earned the Academy Award for Best Actor for his performance. Scorsese was a nominee for best director but did not win. He was, however, presented with the National Society of Film Critics Award for Best Director.

The 1980s were filled with ups and downs for Scorsese. He divorced Rosellini in 1983 and married producer Barbara De Fine in February 1985. That marriage also ended in divorce. He had professional successes with 1985's *After Hours* and 1986's *The Color of Money*, and less well-received films—*The King of Comedy* (1983) and 1988's *The Last Temptation of Christ*, which was criticized by religious groups.

At the beginning of the 1990s, he made *Goodfellas*, a film about the Mafia in New York City. Although the film was violent, Scorsese felt it was violence accurately portrayed and not glorified or candy coated. "It's as realistic as possible, emotionally, and I think that's what was more important about how I felt, because I wasn't going to make it seem pretty—and the reality is this is what happens when a person gets hit in the head, or a person gets hit with a pipe, or somebody gets shot in the chest in a card game. This is the reality. This is what it looks like," he said in 1998. "You may think that the lifestyle of the Goodfellas, for a while, for the first hour of the film, is a lot of exhilaration and fun, but they pay for it for the rest of the film."[8] *Goodfellas* earned Scorsese many awards, including recognition from the National Society of Film Critics, New York Film Critics, and Los Angeles Film Critics.

Scorsese spent the remainder of the 1990s making different kinds of films, including a remake of the thriller *Cape Fear*; an adaptation of Edith Wharton's classic novel *The Age of Innocence*; *Kundun*, a film about the Tibetan spiritual leader, the Dalai Lama; and *Bringing Out the Dead*. He also returned to the mob underground with 1995's *Casino*. In 1997 he received the American Film Institute's Life Achievement Award.

Scorsese married, for the fifth time, in 1999. He and wife, book editor Helen S. Morris, also welcomed their daughter, Francesca, that year.

In addition to a busy personal and professional life, Martin Scorsese believes in preserving film history. In 1990 he became president of the Film Foundation, an organization dedicated to doing just that. After more than twenty films and documentaries, writing numerous screenplays, and bringing a new voice to the film world, Martin Scorsese is determined that his movies and the movies of other great directors and artists are around for future generations to view and reflect on.

He also has a few movies of his own left to make. Martin Scorsese told interviewer Francis Leach in 1998, "I'm really trying to find new ways to tell a story."[9]

7

George Lucas
(1944–)

George Lucas is considered a master storyteller, but, surprisingly, he has only directed five films. However, two of those films include *Star Wars*, which has become one of the highest grossing movies of all time, and the prequel to *Star Wars, Episode One: The Phantom Menace*. He has also been a producer and writer of many movies, including *The Empire Strikes Back, Return of the Jedi*, and *Raiders of the Lost Ark*.

George Lucas was born on May 14, 1944, in Modesto, California, to Dorothy and George Lucas, Sr. George's father owned a successful office supply store and he taught his son and three daughters the value of hard work. But George's dad was convinced his son was not listening to his advice (only years later would he find out that George was taking his

George Lucas

words to heart). "He never listened to me," said George, Sr. "He was his mother's pet. If he wanted a camera, or this or that, he got it. He was hard to understand. He was always dreaming up things."[1]

Part of the younger George's fantasies revolved around his books and he became a lover of history. He enjoyed *Treasure Island, Mutiny on the Bounty,* as well as a series of history books called Landmark Books, which he began reading when he was about eight. "It was from reading these books that I became interested in history—and I never stopped," he later said.[2]

George also liked to build things and was into carpentry, which he did with friends. But even though he was imaginative and loved to read, George was not a very good student. His younger sister, Wendy, often helped him with his papers and his spelling, but George still had a D+ average when he graduated from high school.[3]

In addition to struggling with his studies, George was also the target of neighborhood bullies because he was so small and thin. (He only stands five feet seven inches today.)

As a teenager, George became fascinated with cars and racing. He cruised the streets of Modesto in his car, a Fiat Bianchina, a quick and tiny Italian import. He loved to drive fast on the road he lived on, and his love for speed nearly killed him.

In June 1962, just days before his high school graduation, George had an accident near his home.

He flipped his car, wrapped it around a tree, and was rushed to the hospital. Much to the amazement of his family and doctors, he completely recovered. "The fact that I was alive was a miracle," he later said. "You can't have that kind of experience and not feel that there must be a reason why you're here. I realized that I should be spending my time trying to fulfill it."[4]

For George, that meant going to college and being successful. He did both. After four months of recuperation, he entered Modesto Junior College for two years and then went on to the film school at the University of Southern California (USC).

After he graduated from USC, he went to work as an assistant to Francis Ford Coppola on *Finian's Rainbow*. In 1969, twenty-five-year-old Lucas married film editor Marcia Griffin.

The 1970s were an exciting time for George Lucas. Coppola's company, American Zoetrope, financed his first feature film, *THX 1138*, which was released in 1971. The story, set in the future, was an expanded version of a short film Lucas had won a prize for at USC. The film was not a huge success, but George was not ready to give up.

He next collaborated with Coppola on the 1973 film *American Graffiti*, a film about a group of teenagers in the 1950s, which reminded Lucas of his own teenage years. While the film later proved a huge success, it was an incredibly hard movie to make. With a budget of just $750,000, twenty-eight days to shoot, and a young and inexperienced cast and crew, *American Graffiti* looked like it would never get off the ground. After it was completed and released, the film went on to make $120 million, mostly by positive word of mouth.[5]

But instead of being excited by the success of the film, Lucas nearly quit moviemaking all together.[6] He wanted the kind of creative control that the studios would not allow. He decided to try directing one more picture, the deeply personal *Star Wars*, which he originally envisioned as a trilogy. He had based the character Luke Skywalker on himself. "A lot of stuff in there is very personal," he said. "There's more of me in *Star Wars* than I care to admit. I was trying to say in a simple way, knowing that the film was made for a young audience, that there is a God and there is a good side and a bad side. You have a choice between them, but the world works better if you're on the good side. It's just that simple."[7]

Lucas also made a simple request when negotiating the terms of his contract to make *Star Wars*. Instead of requesting a large amount of cash up front to direct, he asked for ownership of merchandising, music, publishing rights, and sequels. He decided to take a percentage of the profits. It was the smartest financial move he ever made. From his cut of the film alone, Lucas made $40 million.[8]

But he did not do it for the money (he never could have predicted what a huge hit *Star Wars* would be). Instead, he was only trying to protect the

George Lucas's career began when he collaborated with Francis Ford Coppola on *American Grafitti* in 1973. Despite a limited budget and an inexperienced cast and crew, the movie became a huge success.

other parts of the story that he had already written. "I thought it was too wacky for the general public," he later admitted. "I just said, 'Well, I've had my big hit [*American Graffiti*], and I'm happy. And I'm going to do this kind of crazy thing, and it'll be fun, and that will be that.'"[9]

But that was not just that. To say that *Star Wars* was the box-office and critical hit of 1977 would be an understatement. The science-fiction fantasy earned ten Academy Award nominations and became an industry unto itself.[10]

Ironically, after *Star Wars*, George gave up directing for almost twenty years. He did not like directing and he did not like writing, instead seeing himself as a film editor, producer, and businessman. So, with the considerable proceeds from *Star Wars*, George and Marcia formed their own company—Parkway Properties—and bought close to three thousand acres of land in northern California's Marin County. (He now owns six thousand acres.)

This land became Skywalker Ranch, the headquarters of his film company, Lucasfilm, Ltd., as well as housing some of his other enterprises. "It's a creative community," Lucas said. "And me having access to this creative community is what the real dividend of all this is."[11] Today, in addition to office quarters, the community features an estate, stables, three restaurants—even its own fire department![12]

George Lucas continued to write and produce throughout the 1980s, with *Star Wars'* sequels *The*

Empire Strikes Back (1981) and *Return of the Jedi* (1983), as well as the Indiana Jones series of films with his friend Steven Spielberg. As the hits mounted and his fortunes grew, so did his clout in Hollywood.

But for the first time, Lucas was more concerned with other things. In the early 1980s, he and his wife adopted a little girl named Amanda. "Holding that baby was a mystical experience," he said. "It just transformed me from being 99 percent making movies to sort of 30 percent making movies."[13] Although he and Marcia divorced, Lucas adopted two more kids—Katie and Jett—on his own. He put parenting first, and only worked when he felt like he could afford the time away from his children.

Meanwhile, George Lucas's empire continued to grow. He wanted to use technology to advance the art of filmmaking.[14] In addition to Lucasfilms, Ltd., Lucas established Sprocket Systems (a computer postproduction services company); Skywalker Sound (a sound-effects company that also provides digital sound systems licensed under the named THX— after Lucas's first film); and a computer game company called LucasArts Entertainment. He also expanded the special-effects company, Industrial Light and Magic (ILM), which he had created to do the special effects during *Star Wars*. "He has changed the way Hollywood makes movies," said Paul Kagan, a well-known entertainment researcher.[15]

In 1997, for its twentieth anniversary, Lucas rereleased *Star Wars*. He added scenes and enhanced existing ones with digital technology, as well as generating hype for his 1999 release, *Star Wars Episode One: The Phantom Menace*, which he directed after a twenty-year break from the director's chair.

He also directed the second prequel, *Attack of the Clones*, which was released in 2002, and plans to direct the third for release in 2005. "Then, I've got a lot of projects I want to do that are very different from the *Star Wars* films that I've been sort of saving for a long time," George Lucas said.[16] There's no doubt those projects will be just as successful.

Steven Spielberg

Steven Spielberg
(1947–)

When he was thirteen years old, Steven Spielberg was used to being picked on by bullies—one in particular. But he had an idea. Steven wanted to make a movie about World War II. He asked the boy who was bullying him to play a part in *Fighter Squad,* a forty-minute movie he was making with his father's 8-mm camera. The bully became Steven's friend. Steven impressed his friends and teachers with *Fighter Squad,* and they knew he would be famous one day. "He was a filmmaker," his favorite grade-school teacher said. "Always, from the early days."[1]

Steven Spielberg was born on December 18, 1947, the oldest of four children to Arnold and Leah Spielberg. Leah was a concert pianist and Arnold was an electrical engineer who worked on the first computers. His job required that the family move around the country.

Growing up, Steven was influenced by both of his parents' professions. His father encouraged him to study science and math. Steven developed a love for science fiction. His mother wanted her only son to be an artist. Both of his parents' influences can be seen in Spielberg's work today.

Steven was not a very enthusiastic student and he only earned average grades. But he did enjoy school activities. In high school he joined the drama group and played the clarinet in the school orchestra. At first, Steven did not have a lot of friends. But through his filmmaking, just as he had done with the bully, he made friends.

His first feature film was a science-fiction film called *Firelight*, which ran over two hours. Steven wrote the script, cast the actors, filmed the picture, and edited it all by himself. Fifteen-year-old Steven even talked a real movie theater in Phoenix, Arizona, into showing the film, and he ended up making a profit. Steven never looked back. "Once I could make films, I found I could 'create' a great day or a great week just by creating a story; I could synthesize my life. It's just the same reason writers get started, so that they can improve the world or fix it. I found I could do anything or live anywhere via my imagination, through film," Steven said.[2]

He found his escape from reality just in time. When Steven was sixteen, his family moved from

Arizona to California. Shortly after the move, his parents divorced. "That was the worst year of my life," Steven recalled.[3] He had always had a difficult relationship with his dad. He resented the fact that his dad was never home and that the family was always moving around. They grew even more distant after the divorce and hardly spoke for fifteen years.[4]

Steven continued to make movies and was determined to study filmmaking in college. Unfortunately, his grades were poor and he did not get into any college film program. So, in 1967, Spielberg entered California State University at Long Beach as an English major. His new school was near Hollywood, the filmmaking capital, and that was just where Steven wanted to be. In fact, he spent more time cruising the lots and halls at Universal Studios than he did in class.

Throughout his college years, Steven would go to the sound stages, wearing a suit and tie, and visit as many sets as he could. At one point, he even found an empty office, set himself up inside with his name out front, and gave the switchboard operator his extension so he could receive calls. It took the company two years to discover he was there![5] But his perseverance paid off.

Steven managed to convince Universal Studios executive Chuck Silvers to view a short film he had made called *Amblin'*. Silvers and fellow executive Sidney Sheinberg were so impressed that they offered Steven a contract with Universal. There was only one problem—the not yet twenty-one-year-old Spielberg still had a year left of college. Spielberg said that Sheinberg asked him, "'Do you want to be a film director or do you want to get through college?' And I said, 'College? What college?' So I signed a seven-year contract with Universal in 1969."[6]

Spielberg was finally a director. His first project was directing a segment of a television movie called *Night Gallery*. He then filmed episodes of several series including *Marcus Welby, MD.*, *Owen Marshall*, and the pilot (first) episode of the popular series *Columbo*. His work on *Columbo* allowed him to direct his first television movie, *Duel*. The film was so popular in the United States that it was also released in theaters abroad.

As a result of the success of *Duel*, Spielberg directed his first feature film, *The Sugarland Express*, which was based on a true story. It starred Goldie Hawn as part of a couple who try to get their little boy back from his foster family. But it was Spielberg's next film that made him a star. *Jaws* was released in 1975 and despite major production problems and going way over budget, he triumphed and the film became the first to gross over $100 million.

Steven Spielberg was not even thirty years old and he was the director of a blockbuster. He followed it up with another—*Close Encounters of the Third Kind*, a film about people trying to make contact with extraterrestrials. The film earned Spielberg his first Academy Award nomination. It seemed as though he could not make an unsuccessful film, but two year after the release of *Close Encounters*, he released *1941*, a comedy that was panned by critics and did not do well at the box office.

Steven Spielberg did not stay down for long. The 1980s were full of hits for the director. He made *Raiders of the Lost Ark* with friend George Lucas, who produced the film, and earned Spielberg his second Academy Award nomination. The sequels—*Indiana Jones and the Temple of Doom* and *Indiana Jones and the Last Crusade* were nearly as popular as the original.

In 1982, *E. T. The Extra-Terrestrial* took the world by storm. "The movie was manifestation of my feelings about my mom and dad," Spielberg admitted. "The whole movie is really about divorce."[7] But besides a little boy's loneliness, the film is also about friendship, life on other planets, and the wonder of childhood. E.T. became one of the highest-grossing movies of all time.

In 1985, Spielberg married actress Amy Irving and they had a son, Max. In 1989, they divorced. A few years later, Spielberg married another actress, Kate Capshaw. They have seven children in their blended family, between children from previous marriages, adoption, and ones they have had together.

By the mid-1980s, Spielberg had the power to create any movie he wanted in Hollywood. He formed his own production company, Amblin Entertainment, and instead of the fantasy films he'd become famous for, he decided to get serious with

Steven Spielberg's *E. T. The Extra-Terrestrial* was released in 1982 and became one of his highest-grossing movies of all time.

1985's *The Color Purple*, based on the book by Alice Walker. Since then, he has mixed his serious films, such as *Schindler's List, Amistad,* and *Saving Private Ryan* with the fantastical, like *Hook* and *Jurassic Park.* Some of his movies have been tremendous successes while others have been disappointments. But his career as a whole could only be called monumental. As of 2000, his films had grossed more than $2.5 billion.[8] Some of his recent films since then include *A.I. Artificial Intelligence, Shrek,* and *Minority Report.*

In 1987, Spielberg was honored with the Irving G. Thalberg Memorial Award for his contributions to filmmaking. He earned an Oscar for Best Director after the release of his critically acclaimed 1993 film *Schindler's List,* a movie about the Holocaust.

He earned another Oscar for Best Director for the powerful *Saving Private Ryan,* also a film about World War II. The film's star, Tom Hanks, said, "I knew when I saw the movie that Steven had dragged us into something that was much larger than the sum of its parts. I was emotionally crippled by it. I had to sit in my car afterwards. I couldn't even drive."[9] Others have been just as moved by Spielberg's work. In 1995 he received the Life Achievement Award from the American Film Institute.

But Steven Spielberg is not just a filmmaker, he's also a businessman and humanitarian. In 1994 he joined forces with David Geffen and Jeffrey Katzenberg to create the multimedia company DreamWorks SKG (for Spielberg, Katzenberg, and

Geffen). Through the company, he serves as executive producer for many films.

That same year, Spielberg established the nonprofit Survivors of the Shoah Visual History Foundation, dedicated to capturing Holocaust survivors' stories on videotape. He also donated everything he earned from *Schindler's List* to Jewish organizations through the Righteous Persons Foundation.

Steven Spielberg could be called the most successful director of all time, but he remains pretty humble. When asked what he owes his amazing success to, he simply answered, "I sort of know what works."[10]

9

Spike Lee
(1957–)

Indian-American movie director M. Night Shyamalan, who directed 1999's *The Sixth Sense*, said that Spike Lee "gave you the feeling that anyone could [make movies]."[1] By breaking down the barriers of race, Spike Lee gave many minority film directors the chance to follow him inside. Yet, *Entertainment Weekly* writes: "[N]one of his peers can match his commitment to making serious films about race and class and power."[2]

Spike Lee was born Shelton Jackson Lee on March 20, 1957, in Atlanta, Georgia, to Bill and Jacquelyn Lee. His father was an accomplished jazz musician and his mother was a schoolteacher who wanted her children to appreciate black literature and art. Jacquelyn is also credited with giving

Spike Lee

Shelton his nickname "Spike" because he was a tough kid.

Tough kid Spike had a poetic side, though. He liked to read the poetry of Langston Hughes and listen to Miles Davis's music. The family moved to Brooklyn, New York, when Spike was young. When it came time for their five children to enter school, Bill and Jacquelyn gave them a choice: They could attend a largely African-American school or the predominantly white school where their mother taught. Spike chose the predominantly black school.

Later, Spike went on to attend college at his father's alma mater, the all-black Morehouse College. He entered in 1975 and majored in mass communications, but did not have filmmaking aspirations—yet. His first goal was to be the second baseman for the New York Mets.

In 1977, Spike's mom died unexpectedly. His friends tried to cheer him up by taking him to the movies. He became a fan of directors such as Bernardo Bertolucci and Martin Scorsese and movies like *The Deer Hunter*.

That summer, twenty-year-old Spike could not find a summer job, and New York City had a major blackout, which later inspired his 1999 film *Son of Sam*. He bought a Super 8 camera and spent the summer filming his first movie, *Last Hustle in Brooklyn*. His friends and teachers convinced him to pursue his new interest in filmmaking.

After graduation in 1979, Spike Lee entered the Tisch School of Arts graduate film program at New York University (NYU). He made some student films, including the well-received *Joe's Bed-Stuy Barbershop: We Cut Heads*. The forty-five-minute film won him the 1983 Motion Picture Arts and Sciences' Student Academy Award.

But while acclaim was coming his way, money was not rolling in. After he earned his degree, Lee took a job at a film distribution house, cleaning and shipping film. But he had not given up on his dream. He was hoping to get the funds to finance his film *The Messenger*. The money never came and the film was not completed.

Disappointed but wiser for the experience, Spike was determined to make his next flick *She's Gotta Have It*. He had $175,000 and twelve days to make it happen. Because of the constraints of time and money, he even played a character—one of the leading lady's three boyfriends. (He went on to take small roles in many of his films.) *She's Gotta Have It* was released in 1986 and made over $7 million, mainly through art-house runs.

In 1988 he was asked to play the character he created in *She's Gotta Have It* for Nike's Air Jordan commercial campaign. Soon, Lee was directing commercials as well for Levi's, AT&T, ESPN, Taco Bell, Diet Coke, and many more. He opened his own advertising agency, Spike/DDB.

Lee also began directing videos for artists such as Stevie Wonder, Tracy Chapman, and Arrested Development. "I view it all as cinema," he said in 1998. "That's one of the reasons I'm able to navigate from going to different aspects of cinema. To me, I'm a storyteller, and if I look at it like I'm a storyteller, it doesn't seem daunting. I'm going to have a narrative in a 30-second spot, or in a 4-minute music video, or in a feature-length documentary."[3]

The success of his first feature film allowed Lee to make 1988's *School Daze* and 1989's *Do the Right Thing*, both of which he wrote and directed. *School Daze*, a commentary on color discrimination within the black community, earned Lee a reputation as a controversial filmmaker. "I think it's a trap every black artist is faced with," Lee said. "Anytime you do a role or write a novel where some Black people aren't 100-percent angelic, people want to scream you're holding the race back. I try not to get into that debate. . . . To me, the most important thing is to be truthful."[4]

Racial tension was also the theme of *Do the Right Thing*, and Lee was vocal when he felt he was passed over for an Academy Award nomination because of the theme. He even went on the television show *Nightline* to criticize the academy's procedures. He proved he was not afraid of confrontation and would not back down when it came to his beliefs.

Just when critics and audiences thought they could pigeonhole Spike Lee as the angry black director, he switched gears and made a movie about love and music where color did not come into play—*Mo' Better Blues*. "I'm just trying to tell a good story and make thought-provoking, entertaining films," he said of the movie.[5]

But he was right back to his controversial themes with the interracial relationship theme in *Jungle Fever* and 1992's real-life story, *Malcolm X.* A longtime admirer of the slain black leader, Lee was determined to have creative control over the film based on *The Autobiography of Malcolm X* by Alex Haley. Lee had read the book in junior high school and he claimed it changed his life. "Malcolm X is one of the most important people of the 20th century," he said. "We needed time to show the evolution, growth, and many different lives that Malcolm had. His search for truth made him change over and over again. It would be an injustice to his life to take any shortcuts in our film."[6]

Lee took months to research Malcolm's life, because he did not want to take any shortcuts. The finished product was nearly three and a half hours long. "[T]here was so much to tell, and this was not going to be an abbreviated, abridged version of Malcolm X," Lee explained.[7]

The film was a real labor of love for the thirty-five-year-old director. Not only had there been resistance to allowing him to direct the film, but after agreeing to let him direct, the studio would not bankroll him with the $40 million he needed to make the film. They gave him half, and Lee gave up a large portion of his $3 million salary for directing, sold the foreign rights, and asked many black celebrities, including Bill Cosby, Oprah Winfrey, Magic Johnson, and Janet Jackson, to put in money to have the movie made the way he envisioned.

The marketing of *Malcolm X* was even more successful than the film itself. The movie's logo, a bold X, was emblazoned on baseball hats, T-shirts, and posters. Kids were the most likely buyers of the Malcolm merchandise, and Lee had a message for them: He wanted them to skip school to see the PG-13 rated movie (his first non-R rating). Once again, he sparked controversy. "I don't think that it's such a radical idea," he said. "In fourth grade I had to go see *Gone With the Wind* for a class trip and then write a report on the history of the Civil War according to that film. . . . We did not want to give parents nor schoolteachers nor educational systems an excuse why this film cannot be used as a class trip, or why it could not be a part of their curriculum."[8]

Lee's next film, *Crooklyn*, was a personal and autobiographical movie about a black family living in Brooklyn in the 1970s. In the middle of filming, Lee took time off to marry corporate attorney Linette Lewis. The couple has since had two children—a daughter, Satchel, and a son, Jackson.

Lee made many movies in the 1990s, including *Clockers, Girl 6, Get on the Bus, 4 Little Girls* (which was nominated for an Oscar as a Best Documentary

Spike Lee said his movie *Malcolm X* was historically significant. He encouraged educators to use the movie as a learning experience for their pupils.

Feature), *He Got Game,* and *Summer of Sam.* In 2000, Lee made *Bamboozled,* a film about a black minstrel show, and *The Original Kings of Comedy.* He hopes to direct a movie about the life of Jackie Robinson, the first black major-league baseball player.

When he's not writing books (he's written six about filmmaking) or screenplays or directing, Spike Lee loves basketball, specifically the New York Knicks. He even published a book about his love of basketball, *Best Seat in the House: A Basketball Memoir.*

He also enjoys looking for new talent and helping younger filmmakers get their start. He executive produces various projects and teaches third-year students of directing at NYU's film school. He plans to continue taking risks with his films. "You have to take a risk, and a lot of us aren't in a position where we're going to risk giving a hungry, intelligent, but nonetheless inexperienced African-American person a shot. But somebody has to do it. That's how people get breaks."[9]

Quentin Tarantino

10

Quentin Tarantino
(1963–)

Quentin Tarantino was meant to be in the movie business—even before he was born. When his mother was pregnant with him, she saw an episode of *Gunsmoke* and decided to name her unborn child after actor Burt Reynolds's character, Quint.

Quentin Jerome Tarantino was born on March 27, 1963, in Knoxville, Tennessee, to Tony and Connie Tarantino. His father was an amateur musician and his mother was just a teenager when Quentin was born. Connie divorced her husband and took her baby son to California. Quentin never met his father, but Connie remarried. Quentin's stepfather, Curt Zastoupil, was also a musician and he adopted Quentin. Connie eventually became a nurse and then a corporate executive. The family settled in

South Bay, California, a community of many different races and cultures. Connie and Curt divorced when Quentin was nine.

As a child, Quentin loved movies, but he hated school, even though he tested at the genius level with an IQ over 160.[1] The only subject he paid attention to in school was history "because it was kind of like the movies," Quentin recalled.[2]

Quentin's mom allowed her son to watch R-rated movies from a young age, and he was exposed to sexual themes and violence. By the time he was a teenager, Quentin would make a list of every movie he saw. "They would only count if I saw them in the theater, but I'd also count revival houses," Quentin explained. "I would circle the ones I thought were good. Every year, I would have over 200 films on the list."[3]

When he was in his mid-teens, Quentin dropped out of school. His mother's only requirement was that he get a job. He worked as an usher at a movie theater before getting a job at a video store, Video Archives, which fed his hunger to see movies and learn more about them. He also met aspiring film director Roger Avery. The two became friends and writing partners. Quentin started taking acting lessons and writing screenplays. He wrote *True Romance* and *Natural Born Killers* while working at Video Archives.

In 1990 he got a part on the television series *The Golden Girls* as an Elvis impersonator, but he soon decided he'd rather be a director than an actor. He got a job at a small production company in Hollywood, where he managed to get his *True Romance* script read by director Tony Scott. Scott bought it.

In the meantime Tarantino met actor and producer Lawrence Bender. He told Bender his idea for a movie—*Reservoir Dogs*. Bender loved the idea and urged twenty-seven-year-old Tarantino to write it. He did—in three and a half weeks. When Bender read it, he thought: "[T]his is terrific. I told him I thought I could raise some real money for it. I told him I needed a year, and he said I could have two months."[4]

Bender showed the script to his acting teacher, who also had actor Harvey Keitel as a student. The teacher showed Keitel the script and Keitel jumped on board. "I haven't seen characters like these in years," he said.[5]

With Keitel committed to the film, they managed to raise some funds, but still made it on a tight budget. The result was a certified hit. *Reservoir Dogs* made money at the box office when it was released in 1992 and won awards at film festivals, where it shocked audiences with a brutal ten-minute torture sequence.

In 1993, *True Romance* was released, which added to Tarantino's clout in Hollywood. The year 1994 was even bigger for him—he wrote Oliver Stone's film *Natural Born Killers*. But Tarantino had a far bigger hit in 1994 that he managed all on his own—*Pulp Fiction.*

The idea for *Pulp Fiction* started at Video Archives with a script that both Tarantino and Avery had worked on but then shelved. The two shared the piles of screenplay awards the film brought in, including a Golden Globe, an Oscar, and the prestigious Palme d'Or award at the Cannes Film Festival in France. The film won an MTV Award for best picture. Tarantino also won critics' awards for his directing. He said, "*Pulp Fiction* . . . totally delivers on the spills and the chills and the laughs and everything. . . . I don't feel it takes place in the fantasy world at all. I mean part of the fun of it is, it's a depiction of the mundane, right in the criminal world."[6]

Part of that criminal world included a return of actor and 1970s icon John Travolta. Tarantino had always admired the actor, especially from his work in the Brian De Palma films *Carrie* and *Blow Out.* After the actor he had originally cast in the role backed out, Tarantino signed on Travolta. "Quentin told me after he met me that I had haunted him," Travolta later said. "He said, 'I couldn't get you out of my mind for this part. There is a part of your personality that I didn't anticipate, an analytical part I didn't realize you had.'"[7]

Travolta's role in the film was the comeback role he needed, and it started a mutual admiration between the two men. "For others, film is almost a luxury, a hobby that turns into a passion," Travolta said. "For Quentin, film is survival."[8]

Tarantino's survival instincts were good, too. He seemed to be able to sense what audiences would enjoy, whether it was writing, directing, or acting. He has taken small roles in films like *Reservoir Dogs*, *Sleep with Me*, *Pulp Fiction*, *Desperado*, *Four Rooms*, *From Dusk Till Dawn*, and *Little Nicky*.

From 1996 to 1998, Tarantino dated Academy Award-winning actress Mira Sorvino. Their romantic relationship did not work out and Tarantino has yet to get married. However, he would like to find time for more of a personal life.

In 1994 he said, "I want to, like, spend a year. I want to just spend some time, sleeping late, watching films, watching my video, watching my laserdisc. Hang out with my friends. Travel. And then, just kind of, like, organically find it."[9] Fortunately, because he lives modestly in a one-bedroom apartment in West Hollywood, he could have taken the time off and never worried about money. But his career was just taking off.

In 1995, Tarantino codirected and cowrote *Four Rooms*. He also directed the critical hit *Jackie Brown*, starring Pam Grier, another 1970s icon who had disappeared from films until she worked with Tarantino. He is currently rumored to be working on a sequel to *Pulp Fiction*. Hollywood and his fans seem to be anticipating what could be next from one of the most controversial directors working today.

Quentin Tarantino's unique approach to film gained him critical acclaim as one of Hollywood's premier film directors.

Quentin Tarantino has no regrets about breaking the rules and pushing the envelope. "You know, that is always the most exciting time in Hollywood, when they don't know what works anymore. Then they take a chance. First they'll hold on for as long as they can to these old dinosaurs. And then you have a *Pulp Fiction*, a film that doesn't play by the rules yet finds its audience."[10]

Chapter Notes

Introduction

1. John Ashbrook, *The Pocket Essentials Brian De Palma* (Vermont: Trafalgar Square Publishing, 2000), p. 12.

2. Ted Sennett, *Great Movie Directors* (New York: AFI Press, 1986), p. 53.

Chapter 1. Frank Capra

1. Ted Sennett, *Great Movie Directors* (New York: AFI Press, 1986), p. 45.

2. Joseph McBride, *Frank Capra: The Catastrophe of Success* (New York: Simon & Schuster, 1992), p. 19.

3. Ibid., p. 37.

4. Ibid., p. 40.

5. Ibid., p. 43.

6. Ibid., p. 63.

7. Ibid., p. 91.

8. Gary Herman, *The Book of Hollywood Quotes* (London: Ominbus Press, 1979), p. 85.

9. Sennett, p. 45.

10. Jeanine Basinger, *The It's a Wonderful Life Book* (New York: Alfred A. Knopf, 1990), p. ix.

11. Frank Capra, *The Name Above the Title* (New York: The Macmillan Co., 1971), p. 186.

Chapter 2. Alfred Hitchcock

1. Francois Truffaut, *Hitchcock* (New York: Simon & Schuster, 1967), p. 71.

2. Daniel Fierman, *Entertainment Weekly*, "The 100 Greatest Entertainers: 1950-2000," Winter 1999, p. 65.

3. Donald Spoto, *The Dark Side of Genius: The Life of Alfred Hitchcock* (Boston: Little, Brown, & Co., 1983), p. 15.

4. Truffaut, p. 17.

5. Spoto, p. 17.

6. Ibid., p. 32.

7. Truffaut, p. 18.

8. Neil Sinyard, *The Films of Alfred Hitchcock* (New York: Exeter Books, 1986), p. 25.

9. Truffaut, p. 90.

10. Ibid., p. 115.

11. Spoto, p. 319.

12. Ibid., p. 364.

13. Peter Bogdanovich, *Who the Devil Made It* (New York: Alfred A. Knopf, 1997), p. 525.

14. Ibid., p. 473.

15. Fierman, p. 65.

16. Bogdanovich, pp. 473-474.

Chapter 3. Woody Allen

1. Jane Wollman Rusoff, "Woody Allen: He's No Dustin Hoffman," *Mr. Showbiz interview*, December 1, 1995. <http://www.mrshowbiz.go.com/interviews;362_1.html>

2. Neil Sinyard, *The Films of Woody Allen* (New York: Exeter Books, 1987), p. 8.

3. Eric Lax, *Woody Allen* (New York: Alfred A. Knopf, 1991), pp.15-16.

4. Ibid., p. 22.

5. Ibid., p. 20.

6. Ibid., p. 70.

7. Sinyard, p. 10.

8. Ibid., p. 11.

9. Jay Leyda, *Voices of Film Experience* (New York: Macmillan, 1977), p. 5.

10. Lax, p. 181.

11. "The 100 Greatest Entertainers: 1950-2000," *Entertainment Weekly*, Winter 1999, p. 92.

Chapter 4. Francis Ford Coppola

1. Gay Talese, *Esquire*, July 1981, p. 160.

2. Peter Cowie, *Coppola* (1989)

3. Chris Nashawaty, "A Coppola Things," *Entertainment Weekly*, November 21, 1997, p. 57.

4. Ibid.

5. Ibid., p. 56.

6. Carlos Clarens, *Crime Movies: An Illustrated History* (New York: W. W. Norton & Company, 1980), p. 282.

7. Ray Greene, *Mr. Showbiz interview*, August 9, 1996.

8. Fred Ferretti, "Master of Movies and Wine," *Gourmet*, April 1998, p. 62.

9. Ibid., p. 60.

10. "The 100 Greatest Entertainers: 1950-2000," *Entertainment Weekly*, Winter 1999, p. 107.

Chapter 5. Brian De Palma

1. Julie Salamon, *The Devil's Candy: The Bonfire of the Vanities Goes to Hollywood* (Boston: Houghton Mifflin, 1991), p. 29.

2. Ibid., p. 42.

3. Wade Majors, *Mr. Showbiz interview*, August 11, 1998.

4. John Ashbrook, *The Pocket Essentials Brian De Palma* (Vermont: Trafalgar Square Publishing, 2000), p. 16.

5. Ibid., p. 11.

6. Salamon, p. 28.

7. Ibid., p. 388.

8. Majors interview.

9. Ibid.

Chapter 6. Martin Scorsese

1. "The 100 Greatest Entertainers: 1950-2000," *Entertainment Weekly*, Winter 1999, p. 94.

2. Interview with Francis Leach, June 1998.

3. "The 100 Greatest Entertainers: 1950-2000," p. 94.

4. Carlos Clarens, *Crime Movies: An Illustrated History* (New York: W. W. Norton & Company, 1980) p. 325.

5. Roger Ebert, *Roger Ebert's Book of Film* (New York: W. W. Norton & Co., 1997), p. 531.

6. Ibid.

7. Ibid.

8. Interview with Francis Leach, June 1998.

9. Ibid.

Chapter 7. George Lucas

1 Gerald Clarke, "I've Got to Get My Life Back Again," *Time*, May 23, 1983, p. 67.

2. James Friedman and Kate Spelman, "George Lucas, Filmmaker," *TeenInk*, September 2000, p. 26.

3. Dale Pollack, "A Man and His Empire: The Private Life of Star Wars Creator George Lucas," *Life*, June 1983, p. 84.

4. Ibid., p. 87.

5. Randall Lane and James Samuelson, "The Magician," *Forbes*, March 11, 1996, p. 122.

6. Paul Scanlon, "George Lucas Wants to Play Guitar," *Rolling Stone*, July 21, 1983, p. 7.

7. Clarke, p. 66.

8. Lane and Samuelson, p. 125.

9. Bruce Handy, "The Force Is Back," *Time*, February 10, 1997, p. 69.

10. Ted Sennett, *Great Movie Directors* (New York: AFI Press, 1986), p. 159.

11. Lane and Samuelson, p. 125.

12. Ann Armbruster, "Architectural Light & Magic," *Instyle*, April 1999, p. 360.

13. Ibid.

14. Lane and Samuelson, p. 122.

15. Ibid.

16. Friedman and Spelman, p. 28.

Chapter 8. Steven Spielberg

1. Joseph McBride, *Steven Spielberg: A Biography*, (New York: Simon & Schuster, 1997), p. 93.

2. Ibid., p. 94.

3. Robert Sullivan, "Dad Again," *Life*, June 1999, p. 66.

4. Ibid.

5. McBride, p. 109.

6. Judith Crist, *Take 22: Moviemakers on Moviemaking* (New York: Viking, 1984), p. 356.

7. Sullivan, p. 66.

8. Benjamin Svetky, "The 100 Greatest Entertainers: 1950-2000," *Entertainment Weekly*, Winter 1999, p. 31.

9. Ibid., p. 29.

10. Ted Sennett, *Great Movie Directors* (New York: AFI Press, 1986), p. 235.

Chapter 9. Spike Lee

1. "The 100 Greatest Entertainers: 1950-2000," *Entertainment Weekly*, Winter 1999, p. 140.

2. Ibid.

3. Anthony Vagnoni, "Spike: It's Not Just About Control, It's About the Creative Process," *Advertising Age*, June 1998, p. 20.

4. Jill Nelson, "Mo' Better Spike," *Essence*, August 1990, pp. 106-108.

5. Ibid., p. 106.

6. *Scholastic Update*, "Spike Goes the Extra Mile for Malcolm," October 23, 1992, p. 18.

7. Janice C. Simpson, "Words with Spike," *Time*, November 23, 1992, p. 66.

8. Ibid., p. 66.

9. Henry Louis Gates, Jr., "Spike Lee: The Do-the-Right-Thing Revolution," *Interview*, October 1994, p. 156.

Chapter 10. Quentin Tarantino

1. Anne Thompson, "I'm as Serious as a Heart Attack," *Entertainment Weekly*, November 4, 1994, p. 36.

2. Ibid.

3. Ibid.

4. Rod Lurie, "Natural Born Killer," *Los Angeles Magazine*, October 1994, p. 66.

5. Ibid.

6. "A Conversation with Quentin Tarantino," *Newsweek*, December 26, 1994, p. 119.

7. Lurie, p. 66.

8. Ibid.

9. Thompson, p. 36.

10. "A Conversation with Quentin Tarantino," p. 119.

Further Reading

Adair, Gene. *Alfred Hitchcock: Filming Our Fears.* New York: Oxford University Press, 2002.

Cross, Robin. *Movie Magic: A Behind-the-Scenes Look at Filmmaking.* New York: Sterling Publishing Company, 1996.

Haskins, Jim. *Spike Lee: By Any Means Necessary.* New York: Walker & Co., 1997.

Powers, Tom. *Steven Spielberg: Master Storyteller.* Minneapolis: Lerner Publications, 1997.

Smith, Dian G. *Great American Film Directors.* New York: Simon & Schuster, 1987.

Woog, Adam. *George Lucas.* San Diego: Lucent Books, 2000.

Internet Addresses

Alfred Hitchcock:
<http://www.hitchcock-collection.com>

Brian De Palma:
<http://www.briandepalma.net/>

Frank Capra:
<http://www.geocities.com/Hollywood/Makeup/8156/
     frankcapra.htm>

George Lucas:
<http://www.starwars.com/bio/georgelucas.html>

Spike Lee:
<http://www.eonline.com/Facts/People/Bio/0,128,9175,00.
     html>

Steven Spielberg:
<http://www.spielberg-dreamworks.com>

Index